G000077762

Life's a Beach

summersdale

LIFE'S A BEACH

Summersdale Publishers Ltd
46 West Street
Chichester
West Sussex
PO19 1RP
UK

www.summersdale.com

Printed and bound in the Czech Republic

ISBN: 978-1-78685-352-3

Substantial discounts on bulk quantities of Summersdale books are available to corporations, professional associations and other organisations. For details contact general enquiries: telephone: +44 (0) 1243 771107, fax: +44 (0) 1243 786300 or email: enquiries@summersdale.com.

TO: *Molly*

FROM: *Ella*

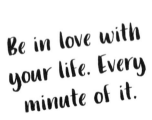

Be in love with your life. Every minute of it.

Jack Kerouac

KEEP SMILING, BECAUSE LIFE IS A BEAUTIFUL THING AND THERE'S SO MUCH TO SMILE ABOUT.

Marilyn Monroe

BE HAPPY AND TRUTHFUL AND LIFE WILL BE FRUITFUL

Live in the
sunshine,
swim in the
sea, drink in
the wild air.

Ralph Waldo Emerson

life is to be
enjoyed, not
just endured.

Gordon B. Hinckley

EXPLORE, DREAM, DISCOVER.

H. Jackson Brown Jr

EMBRACE
YOUR INNER
'GLAMINGO'

This life is not for complaint, but for satisfaction.

Henry David Thoreau

Turn your face
to the sun and
the shadows fall
behind you.

Maori proverb

THE SOUL'S JOY
LIES IN DOING.

Percy Bysshe Shelley

Seas
the day!

LIFE IS A GREAT BIG CANVAS, AND YOU SHOULD THROW ALL THE PAINT ON IT YOU CAN.

Danny Kaye

YOU ARE NEVER TOO LATE TO SET ANOTHER GOAL OR DREAM A NEW DREAM.

Les Brown

One
cannot
have too
large a
party.

Jane Austen

LAUGHTER IS AN INSTANT VACATION.

Milton Berle

WHEREVER YOU GO, NO MATTER WHAT THE WEATHER, ALWAYS BRING YOUR OWN SUNSHINE.

Anthony J. D'Angelo

live for
the 'wow'
moments
all the
time

Look at
everything
as though you
were seeing it
for the first or
last time.

Betty Smith

LIFE ISN'T ABOUT WAITING FOR THE STORM TO PASS; IT'S ABOUT LEARNING TO DANCE IN THE RAIN.

Anonymous

Tropic like
it's hot!

THE WORLD IS ALWAYS OPEN, WAITING TO BE DISCOVERED.

Dejan Stojanović

BE GLAD OF LIFE
BECAUSE IT GIVES
YOU THE CHANCE TO
LOVE, TO WORK, TO
PLAY AND TO LOOK
UP AT THE STARS.

Henry van Dyke

Be content
with what
you have.

Lao Tzu

Watch
more
sunsets
than
boxsets

LIKING WHAT YOU DO IS HAPPINESS.

Frank Tyger

IT IS ONLY POSSIBLE TO LIVE HAPPILY EVER AFTER ON A DAY-TO-DAY BASIS.

Margaret Bonanno

Enjoy the journey of life with all its twists and turns

Too much of a
good thing can
be wonderful.

Mae West

EVERY DAY BRINGS A CHANCE FOR YOU TO DRAW IN A BREATH, KICK OFF YOUR SHOES... AND DANCE.

Oprah Winfrey

Don't go
through
life, grow
through life.

Eric Butterworth

WILD,
BAREFOOT
AND FREE

OPPORTUNITIES DON'T OFTEN COME ALONG. SO, WHEN THEY DO, YOU HAVE TO GRAB THEM.

Audrey Hepburn

Laughter is
a tranquiliser
with no
side effects.

Arnold H. Glasow

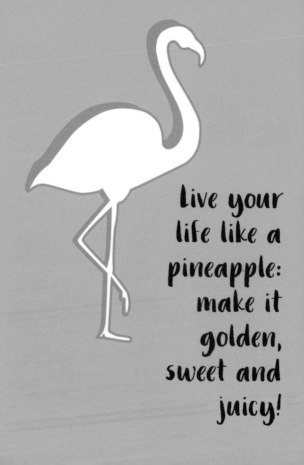

Live your life like a pineapple: make it golden, sweet and juicy!

THE GOOD LIFE IS ONE INSPIRED BY LOVE AND GUIDED BY KNOWLEDGE.

Bertrand Russell

WHOEVER IS HAPPY WILL MAKE OTHERS HAPPY TOO.

Anne Frank

There is little success where there is little laughter.

Andrew Carnegie

Today is a
blank page –
what are you
going to write
on it?

THE WAY TO KNOW
LIFE IS TO LOVE
MANY THINGS.

Vincent Van Gogh

Laugh, and the world laughs with you.

Ella Wheeler Wilcox

HIGH TIDES =
GOOD VIBES

LIFE IS A HELLUVA LOT MORE FUN IF YOU SAY 'YES' RATHER THAN 'NO'.

Richard Branson

Why not just live in the moment, especially if it has a good beat?

Goldie Hawn

Life is either
a daring
adventure
or nothing.

Helen Keller

TAKE SOMETHING POSITIVE FROM EVERY SITUATION

YOU ONLY GET ONE CHANCE AT LIFE AND YOU HAVE TO GRAB IT BOLDLY.

Bear Grylls

Why did
we wait for
anything? –
why not seize
the pleasure
at once?

Jane Austen

When life hands you pineapples, make pina coladas

LIVE SIMPLY.
DREAM BIG.
BE GRATEFUL.
GIVE LOVE.
LAUGH LOTS.

Anonymous

Every day
holds the
possibility of
a miracle.

Elizabeth David

MAY YOU LIVE
EVERY DAY
OF YOUR LIFE.

Jonathan Swift

ANYTHING
FLAMIN-GOS

Opportunity dances with those who are already on the dance floor.

H. Jackson Brown Jr

It's never too late – never too late to start over, never too late to be happy.

Jane Fonda

KEEP CHASING
THAT SUN OF
A BEACH

THE SUN IS NEW
EACH DAY.

Heraclitus

If you look the right way, you can see that the whole world is a garden.

Frances Hodgson Burnett

If we had
no winter,
the spring
would not be
so pleasant.

Anne Bradstreet

YOUR LIFE IS A WORK OF ART – BE PROUD TO DISPLAY IT

Live, travel, adventure, bless, and don't be sorry.

Jack Kerouac

FEELINGS ARE MUCH LIKE WAVES – WE CAN'T STOP THEM FROM COMING, BUT WE CAN CHOOSE WHICH ONES TO SURF.

Jonatan Mårtensson

SUN, SAND AND A PINEAPPLE IN HAND

Laugh as if it's funny, embrace as if it's love, and smile anyway.

Richelle E. Goodrich

A day
without
laughter
is a day
wasted.

Nicolas Chamfort

LET NOTHING HOLD YOU BACK!

ONE JOY SCATTERS
A HUNDRED GRIEFS.

Chinese proverb

Laughter is
a sunbeam
of the soul.

Thomas Mann

Think less,
live more

OUR LIFE IS WHAT OUR THOUGHTS MAKE IT.

Marcus Aurelius

Humour is the
great thing, the
saving thing.

Mark Twain

HAPPINESS IS NOT SOMETHING READY-MADE. IT COMES FROM YOUR OWN ACTIONS.

Dalai Lama

DOSE
YOURSELF
UP WITH SOME
VITAMIN SEA

Happiness often sneaks in through a door you didn't know you left open.

John Barrymore

Live the life
you have
imagined.

Henry David Thoreau

LIFE IS SWEET
– TAKE A
BIG BITE!

WHAT WE DO TODAY IS WHAT MATTERS MOST.

Buddha

The sea,
once it's
cast its
spell, holds
one in its
net forever.

Jacques Cousteau

The
moments of
happiness we enjoy
take us by surprise.
It is not that we
seize them, but
that they seize us.

Ashley Montagu

FIND THE
BEAUTY IN
EVERYDAY
THINGS

Happy
people plan
actions.

Denis Waitley

TENSION IS WHO YOU THINK YOU SHOULD BE; RELAXATION IS WHO YOU ARE.

Chinese proverb

HELLO PALM TREES AND WARM BREEZE

Happiness is
not a station
you arrive at,
but a manner
of travelling.

Margaret Lee Runbeck

May your trails be crooked, winding... leading to the most amazing view.

Edward Abbey

**SURROUND
YOURSELF WITH
ONLY PEOPLE
WHO ARE GOING
TO LIFT YOU
UP HIGHER.**

Oprah Winfrey

GO OUT THERE AND GRAB LIFE!

Anxiety
is the
dizziness
of freedom.

Søren Kierkegaard

If you've got nothing to dance about, find a reason to sing.

Melody Carstairs

HAPPY MIND, HAPPY LIFE

There are
always
flowers for
those who
want to
see them.

Henri Matisse

MIX A LITTLE FOOLISHNESS WITH YOUR SERIOUS PLANS.

Horace

LAUGHTER IS THE SOUND OF THE SOUL DANCING.

Jarod Kintz

Sandy toes,
sun-kissed
nose

Where
there is
love there
is life.

Mahatma Gandhi

CARRY LAUGHTER
WITH YOU
WHEREVER
YOU GO.

Hugh Sidey

BE AS FREE AS
THE OCEAN

I think
that beauty
comes from
being happy
and connected
to the people
we love.

Marcia Cross

Wherever you go,
go with all
your heart.

Confucius

ENTHUSIASM MOVES THE WORLD.

Arthur Balfour

Replace
the word
'challenge'
with
'opportunity'

ONE WAY TO GET THE MOST OUT OF LIFE IS TO LOOK UPON IT AS AN ADVENTURE.

William Feather

LAUGHTER TO ME
IS BEING ALIVE.

William Saroyan

If there's a
will there's
a wave

Happiness
is a way of
travel, not a
destination.

Roy M. Goodman

DREAM AS IF YOU'LL LIVE FOREVER. LIVE AS IF YOU'LL DIE TODAY.

James Dean

THE PURPOSE OF DANCING – AND OF LIFE – IS TO ENJOY EVERY MOMENT AND EVERY STEP.

Wayne W. Dyer

Make
every
day
count

The greatest
pleasure of life
is love.

Euripides

LIFE IS SHORT.
KISS SLOWLY,
LAUGH INSANELY,
LOVE TRULY AND
FORGIVE QUICKLY.

Paulo Coelho

Life is not
a dress
rehearsal –
enjoy your
time in the
limelight!

NOTHING TO ME
FEELS AS GOOD
AS LAUGHING
INCREDIBLY HARD.

Steve Carell

DON'T COUNT THE DAYS; MAKE THE DAYS COUNT.

Anonymous

The only reason
to be alive is
to enjoy it.

Rita Mae Brown

Be
footloose
and
fancy-free!

IF YOU HAVE GOOD
THOUGHTS THEY
WILL SHINE OUT OF
YOUR FACE LIKE
SUNBEAMS AND
YOU WILL ALWAYS
LOOK LOVELY.

Roald Dahl

ENJOY THE LITTLE
THINGS, FOR ONE
DAY YOU MAY LOOK
BACK AND REALISE
THEY WERE THE
BIG THINGS.

Robert Brault

Don't
shrink
from a
challenge
– embrace
it!

Every
moment is
a fresh
beginning.

T. S. Eliot

LIFE IS NOT
MEASURED BY THE
NUMBER OF BREATHS
YOU TAKE, BUT BY
THE MOMENTS
THAT TAKE YOUR
BREATH AWAY.

Anonymous

There is nothing in the world so irresistibly contagious as laughter and good humour.

Charles Dickens

BEACH DAYS
EVERY DAY

THE MAN THAT LOVES AND LAUGHS MUST SURE DO WELL.

Alexander Pope

Your attitude
is like a box
of crayons
that colour
your world.

Allen Klein

Don't save
things for
a special
occasion. Every
day of your
life is a special
occasion.

Anonymous

DON'T RACE
FOR THE
FINISH LINE
– ENJOY THE
JOURNEY

DO ANYTHING,
BUT LET IT
PRODUCE JOY.

Henry Miller

Believe
and act as
if it were
impossible
to fail.

Charles Kettering

Be happy
with what you
have and are, be
generous with both,
and you won't
have to hunt for
happiness.

William Gladstone

MAKE
YOUR OWN
SUNSHINE!

Those who
bring sunshine
into the lives
of others cannot
keep it from
themselves.

J. M. Barrie

IF YOU ASK ME WHAT
I CAME INTO THIS
LIFE TO DO, I WILL
TELL YOU: I CAME
TO LIVE OUT LOUD.

Émile Zola

TELL ME, WHAT
IS IT YOU PLAN
TO DO WITH YOUR
ONE WILD AND
PRECIOUS LIFE?

Mary Oliver

Stay salty
for days

Look at life
through the
windshield,
not the rear-
view mirror.

Byrd Baggett

NOTHING IS WORTH MORE THAN THIS DAY.

Johann Wolfgang von Goethe

FIND ECSTASY IN LIFE; THE MERE SENSE OF LIVING IS JOY ENOUGH.

Emily Dickinson

Don't wait for good things to happen – go out and get them!

There are
exactly as many
special occasions in
life as we choose
to celebrate.

Robert Brault

THIS VERY MOMENT IS A SEED FROM WHICH THE FLOWERS OF TOMORROW'S HAPPINESS GROW.

Margaret Lindsey

My sun
sets to
rise again.

Robert Browning

HAVE
NO REGRETS

EACH DAY COMES BEARING ITS OWN GIFTS. UNTIE THE RIBBONS.

Ruth Ann Schabacker

Life isn't a matter of milestones, but of moments.

Rose Kennedy

Live life to
the fullest,
and focus on
the positive.

Matt Cameron

BEACH,
PLEASE!

THE FUTURE BELONGS TO THOSE WHO BELIEVE IN THE BEAUTY OF THEIR DREAMS.

Eleanor Roosevelt

This life is
what you
make it.

Marilyn Monroe

Life keeps throwing me lemons because I make the best lemonade.

King James Gadsden

KEEP
CALM AND
TROPICANA
ON

Look up
to the sky.
You'll never
find rainbows
if you're
looking down.

Charlie Chaplin

BELIEVE THAT LIFE
IS WORTH LIVING,
AND YOUR BELIEF
WILL HELP CREATE
THE FACT.

William James

IT'S MORE FUN TO THINK OF THE FUTURE THAN DWELL ON THE PAST.

Sara Shepard

Every
second
is of
infinite
value.

Johann Wolfgang von Goethe

IF YOU LOVE LIFE, LIFE WILL LOVE YOU BACK.

Arthur Rubinstein

If you're interested in finding out more about our books, find us on Facebook at **Summersdale Publishers** and follow us on Twitter at **@Summersdale**.

www.summersdale.com